Cats

an Illustrated
Teach Yourself book

Illustrated
Teach Yourself

Cats

Will Green

 Knight
Books

ISBN 0 340 19602 5

This edition published 1975 by Knight Books, the
paperback division of Brockhampton Press Ltd, Leicester
First published in 1974 by Brockhampton Press Ltd
Text copyright © 1974 Brockhampton Press Ltd
Photographs copyright © 1974 Will Green
Line drawing (pages 66–8) by Leslie Marshall
copyright © 1970 Brockhampton Press Ltd

Printed in Belgium by Henri Proost & Cie, Turnhout

Contents

Acquiring a kitten
or a cat

Why a cat? Why do you want a cat for a pet? You know what makes one animal different from another and you probably know which kind is best for you. Why then choose a cat?

When anyone decides to have a pet, it may be the result of much waiting and looking and hoping. Or it may be the result of pleading and suggesting by a child or friend. If there has been real heart searching, this is as it should be, for it is most important to the pet that it has been taken into your home because you really want it and understand your responsibilities to it. To acquire a pet in a rush of emotion and excitement is not often a good idea for, if love only lasts as long as novelty and interest, then the rest of the cat's life will be miserable.

Cats and children When an adult wants to give a pet to a child, it is most important to make sure, not only that the child really wants it, but also that the adults in the background will supervise the care of the cat.

Personally, I dislike giving animals as surprise Christmas or birthday presents unless the yearning for the pet is already there. In any case, it is better to let the recipient choose his own kitten from the litter.

Strays You may take in a stray because you are sorry for it. This can work out well enough but it is still true that you must keep it because you *want* it, with all its probable faults and possible fleas. Otherwise, find a home for it elsewhere or get in touch with one of the animal welfare societies.

Companions Old people sometimes want cats as companions and, of course, for the less active, this can avoid many hours of loneliness. For active old people, however, a cat is rarely the right choice. It will not accompany them on a walk across the fields, follow them to the shops or guard their possessions like a dog. A cat is a fairly sedentary creature and will amply return any affection it is offered. It can be an excellent companion – on its own terms.

Of course, you might wish to breed from your pet or enter it in shows. Nevertheless, the main reason must be that you *want that cat*. You must be willing to understand the lovely qualities of cats, how to avoid giving them twists of character and behaviour which will be unlikable, and how to make them as happy as you hope they will make you.

Acquiring a kitten Sometimes not enough trouble is taken in the choosing of a kitten for a pet. Most people seem to go into a shop or a friend's house and say, 'I'll have that one' without much thought, or perhaps accept one offered by someone too willing to be rid of it. It is better to look round for a while before taking on the responsibility and to find the one that really appeals. Acquiring a kitten is a little like having a new baby in the house. As far as the kitten is concerned it will be a total and unexpected change in its life; it will be a change in yours, too, if this is your first kitten.

What kind of kitten? On this will partly depend the source from which you get it. There are so many varieties – long-haired or short; white, tabby or coloured; male or female; mixed breed or pedigree. Each has something special about it and you must decide this first. A long-haired kitten will have to be helped with its grooming and you will be faced with the unexpected regurgitated fur ball dropping on the floor, anywhere indoors – not very pleasant but not serious. On the other hand, a long-haired cat is often more attractive, more cuddly for a child. Many are pedigree cats. Short-haired cats groom themselves more easily and fleas are more readily detected and eliminated.

Where do you live? The area where you live might affect your choice. In an industrial environment, or near demolition sites, a cat that roams gets off-colour very easily. In the country even a long-haired white cat stays that way as a rule.

A tabby cat shows dirt less, a black cat shows dirt of a different kind from a white cat. Either a white or a black cat looking grey is a dowdy sight. These are important considerations.

Male or female? The sex does not matter so much if you intend to have the cat neutered but otherwise certain characteristics of both may or may not appeal to you. I think females make better pets because they stay at home rather more than males. Toms love to wander round the neighbourhood and sometimes stay away for days on end. Of course, toms do not produce kittens so you may want a female for that reason.

My choice My own first choice would be for a short-haired silver tabby, not a pedigree but a pet; or a female golden tabby or alternatively, if well marked, a torty-&-white, perhaps with medium-length hair.

For breeding? If you want a kitten from which you will eventually breed pedigree cats, or which you want to put into shows, or a pedigree for any other reason, you will obviously choose the breed first, then seek the source. My advice is to find the nearest local regular breeder of

9

A ginger and white kitten alert and wide-eyed

repute. You will be able to go back to him if you have a complaint or a query. Such a breeder would guard his reputation by giving little cause for one and being helpful with the other. The many cat clubs all over the country will advise about local breeders. The National Cat Club can help in a general way but would probably redirect you to a list of known breeders, or to a club which caters specifically for the breed you prefer. A list of cat clubs and breed clubs is on pages 92-4. Successes at local shows and the advertisements in the schedules of cat shows or in animal magazines will also guide you.

Just a pet If you simply want a kitten and, apart from some personal preferences, do not mind what it is so long as it is a pet, there are many sources. The best is probably a personal friend who will let you see the kittens several times before making a choice. One would not choose a kitten from a poor litter, or from a suspect cat, or from a suspect person. If you can see it developing for a week or two, you may be fairly sure that you have a healthy kitten and that you have selected the one you really prefer. It is almost like falling in love. Unfortunately, friends' cats do not always produce kittens at the time you want one, so you may be looking for another reliable source. You are faced with a problem.

Try a pet shop Many pet shops are totally reliable and so are the various animal welfare clinics. Vets are sometimes asked to accept a kitten and find a home for it, though they are not usually willing to do so. They may take an address, however.

Pet shops are likely to have more kittens at weekends. People who wish to dispose of kittens are asked to bring them in towards the end of the week – especially after early closing day. More kittens are sold at weekends and the shops do not want to have to keep them longer than necessary. Such kittens may be quite acceptable but one does take a chance. A good shop, run by people who care about animals, will probably inspect for defects. I have heard of shops asking for a vet's note before accepting animals. Certainly, if you buy a kitten from a shop and it proves to be ill within a day or two you should be able to take it back, so long as you can be sure it was ill when you bought it. If you do return it, however, it is more than likely that the shopkeeper will have it put down to avoid any infection spreading.

A good shop will supply good kittens and will readily give advice on feeding, at least concerning tinned and prepared food. If you buy from a pet shop, it will probably sell the various things you need, such as a brush, basket and general medicaments. It is worth while to make a friend of the owner. He will want to keep your custom and so will give you the benefit of his experience.

It is a good idea to have your kitten examined by a vet at once and make friends with him, too. He will want to help you to keep your cat happy.

Other sources Children might come to your door asking if you can find a home for a stray kitten they are carrying. They may have picked it up near to its home, thinking it is a stray, and then try to find a home for it, or sell it. It is wise to see their parents before taking a chance on their offering.

This situation often happens to me as it is well known that I have had many cats. Sometimes the kitten is clean and well fed – not a stray at all but one which has simply wandered out of its home. It is better to look for the owner. I have taken in several of these 'strays' and am glad to say homes were soon found for them – sometimes the owner appeared on my doorstep.

Street markets are not good places to buy pets. Stolen kittens are sometimes traded there although, having said this, I must admit that one of my first cats originated in East Lane, Walworth. She was a lovely cat and one of the best pets and friends one could hope for.

Kittens turn into cats How can you tell which kitten will make the best cat? Although she may now be a lovely, lovable, cuddly

Showing the haws of the eyes means that something is wrong with the cat

bundle of fur, so teasily playful and appealing, one day your kitten will be a large, slow, stealthy, heavy, quiet, self-centred, full-grown *cat*. You might get some indication of how she will turn out if you know her parents, or the general tendencies of the breed; or the owner of the mother might tell you what kind of kittens have previously resulted from this cat and her mates.

Choosing the one you want Having decided which qualities you would like in theory, how can you choose from among the many kittens you will see?

Choosing for breeding or showing will be a specialist's job and only a specialist in the particular breed can guide you. However, there are some points to look for in general terms, whatever kind of kitten you want.

First, the kitten must *look* healthy. It will not pretend to be well if it does not feel well, nor ill if it is fit. Look at its eyes; they should be bright and alive. Do they sparkle and look straight at you? Allow for the fact that it may be overawed by being in the hands of a stranger.

A cat has two special eye-lids which sometimes close

or half-close when the cat is unwell or very uncertain of itself. These are called the haws and are sloping pink skin-like lids situated at the bottom corner near the nose, inside the normally furry lids. If the haws show, you should beware though it is not always a sign that anything is very wrong. When reassured, or held by a friend, the haws should disappear and the eyes brighten. Sometimes, a healthy but very tired cat will show its haws. If they do not go down readily, do not accept the animal. It is an indication that something is not quite right.

A kitten's spirit and eagerness to fight your hand is interesting. It is better to take a kitten that spits at you than one which cowers. It is better still to find one that looks you full in the eyes, slaps your finger with its paw and backs away, then runs back at you; or bites you playfully. Without frightening it, offer it your hand. It is preferable to watch all the kittens from a short distance first. Does the kitten run well and do its limbs move evenly? If it is very young it may wobble but it should wobble evenly, not limp. Does it stick its tail straight up when it is running in play? Does it flick its tail in playful anger when it fights another kitten? It should. Handle the kitten. Is its fur clean and does it feel even when you run your fingers over it? Can you open the paws easily and see the tiny claws? Does it wince or mew when you touch any part of it? Brush its fur against the grain and see whether there are any specks of black in the roots – the tell-tale specks left by fleas. Look for fleas under the armpits, under the groins, under the chin, by brushing up the fur slowly and re-leasing it a bit at a time. Fleas on kittens can be eradi-cated fairly easily; the seller should do this for you overnight.

Sexing   Now lift the tail and determine its sex. In very young kittens, under two weeks, it is not always easy to tell the sex immediately but such young kittens are not ready to be taken from their mother. By four or five weeks, the bump of the testicles of the male is quite obvious and, even among longish fur, can be felt easily. The female has a crinkled slit below the anus – like two

anuses, in fact; this is quite obvious even among long fur.

Males tend to be slightly heavier but this is not a sure sign. Females tend to look daintier and prettier but, again, this is not a sure sign. Look under the tail firmly but without being rough. Make sure you examine it properly. It is the time to be practical.

Next, examine the kitten all over. One of my cats was unfortunate enough to produce a kitten with a dislocated paw which I did not discover for several weeks. By that time, the vet said it was permanently deformed but, as the kitten was not uncomfortable and had learned to live with this curiously-shaped leg, it would be wiser not to interfere. In fact, a willing owner was found and the kitten proved to be an excellent member of the family. Since then I have examined every kitten born in my house within an hour or two of birth.

How old? What is the correct age to transfer a kitten? Some say five weeks, others say ten. I have always made sure that a kitten could feed well and groom itself before passing it to a new owner. I think you should see it eating and drinking with ease before accepting it. Many a kitten can struggle through from about six weeks but the comfort of its mother, who may still wish to feed it, is still important. A mother's last kitten should not be taken away from her until she has finished feeding, or she will be very distressed.

My advice is to wait until about the eighth week. By then it should be able to cope and its mother will not mind. Also, it can come to terms with you among all the other difficulties it might have to face.

Its new home You should have already made arrangements to receive your pet. A box or basket, softly lined, a feeding bowl with its normal food, a dish of milk and warmth should all be waiting.

The kitten should be carried home in a box or basket from which it definitely cannot escape. It is surprising how cleverly these feline Houdinis can wriggle through small holes in boxes, between cracks of half-tied-down lids, half-zipped-up bags. It must realise that it cannot get out, for if it thinks that there is a possibility, it will become desperate to try. At the same time it must not be made afraid and should feel safe, warm and cosy in the box. Useful and stout pet-carrying boxes can be bought for less than a pound but even these are not entirely cat-proof.

When you get it home If it is a lively kitten, or if it is somewhat afraid, it may fly out of the basket as soon as it is opened, run wild, and then hide in some place where, for weeks afterwards, it will tend to vanish every time it wants to hide. It is better to leave the box in the room with the lid still on, or the basket still closed. Shut the door and

The age of your kitten

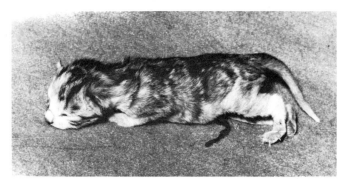

a

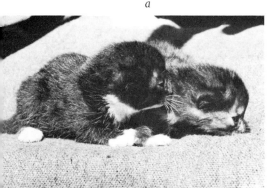

b

c

d

a   A few hours old
b   8–10 days old
c   4 weeks old
d   5–6 weeks old
e   8 weeks old

e

window, place food and its own things near-by and wait quietly.

Then open the lid. If the kitten gets out itself, let it find its own way around. If not, lift it out gently and put it into its sleeping box or basket at once. There should be no rush of children to squeal and fuss over it, or it may vanish under a cupboard, behind books on a shelf, or up the curtains. Talk to it gently as it wanders about. The more free it feels to do what it wants, the sooner it will trust you and make friends. Your new life together has begun.

How to tell ages   How can you tell that a kitten you are offered is in fact old enough to be separated from its mother, unless you see it feed and groom itself? How can you judge the age of a stray? You cannot tell exactly but there are a few signs to look out for which will help you to make an approximate judgment.

Ears   Until about four weeks these are rounded, furry, fluffy and pressed forward and down. At five or six weeks they prick up a little, become sharper and slightly harder in outline. By six or seven weeks they are less thickly furred and the kitten moves them easily to

This kitten, about six weeks old, shows the fighting ridge running along its spine from neck to tail. It is only moderately upstanding in this picture

listen to you, or to avoid your flicking finger. Try tickling a hair protruding from inside. The kitten should close the ear down and backwards or flick it sharply.

Eyes These lose their baby look at about three or four weeks and become more positive. At four to five weeks they look at you with interest, not merely in your direction. They lose their slight look of apprehension. At six to seven weeks they can almost communicate; the eyes laugh, get worried, show amazement and anger. Usually blue at first, colour appears at widely varying ages from four to ten weeks.

Tail At birth, tails are short and tapered; at about three to four weeks they seem to fluff out a little with thin fur, which is often thinner underneath. By five to six weeks they have more parallel sides, are more snaky and active. By eight weeks they really are tails and have become a means of communication. Watch them waggle, or spin round, or flick from side to side. Tail-flicking in fun-fights starts at about four to five weeks.

General From a very early age, kittens literally get their backs up when fighting. When a cat is wildly angry, aggressive and, perhaps, even in a panic, the hairs along its spine stand erect, forming a ridge from neck to tail. This is called the fighting ridge. It rarely appears before five to six weeks and then, only when in panic or in defiance. They run forwards *and* backwards from about three to four weeks. At about four weeks they easily jump forwards, with all feet off the floor at once. By six weeks they jump over things and even jump or run sideways. In fights they present a broadside view to opponents. Kittens do not bite much until about four or five weeks but by eight weeks they bite without compunction. In fact, by eight weeks they do every physical thing they can; jump, roll, somersault, growl, stand on hind-legs, even jump from a height of five or six feet.

Taking an adult cat into your home is a very different thing from acquiring a young kitten. Cats soon get set in their ways and attach themselves to people and places. Early in life a cat begins to think that the way of life he has been following so far is the way things are and always will be. Any major change in that routine can be a shattering experience for a nervous adult cat and can alter his whole character or at least upset his social behaviour. If he meets what appears to him an upheaval in his life, he might go stray or even become a rogue.

A properly educated cat, on the other hand, will change its home and even its owner with little trouble, even if it misses its first home or owner for a long time.

There is some truth in the story that a cat will always find its way back to its old home, but why does it bother? If it is happy in its new home it will not try to return to old haunts. I believe a happy cat should never want to go back to a previous home. It may set off and not reach there – and may never be heard of again.

Your first task with your new cat must be to convince him that you are to be trusted, that you are as friendly and affectionate as his previous owner and that he will enjoy living with you. If possible, get to know the cat before the transfer and let the cat get to know you well. To make him accept you as a friend give him something to eat, fondle him and talk to him, using his name.

Let his previous owner carry him to your home and be there when the basket or box is opened – and stay for a while afterwards. Transfer with him as much of his old home as is practicable, even if it is to be kept for only a short time, such as his sleeping box and blanket. Let him see his own feeding bowls, litter box, brush and comb and any toys he likes.

Fondle him and talk to him again in your home and offer him tit-bits of his favourite food. Be gentle, be quiet. Keep him indoors for a few days, preferably in one or two rooms with a litter box, and only open the door to the outside world when you are sure you have won his trust. If he claws at the doors and windows constantly, mewing to go out or tries to get through the door with you, on no account allow him to do so. You have not won him round. You have not made him happy. With patience and kindness you will win him over.

Do not feed him for a while before you eventually open the door. Leave him in a room with the door or window open to a garden or yard where he can go to explore and play. Rattle his bowl or fishpan and he will stay within earshot of this, and you can call him back to it when you are ready. Within two or three days, he will not roam at all. You and his new home will be accepted.

The cat's home

Your home is the cat's home, or at least the greater
part of it is. Just as you might like to feel that one place
in the house is specially yours, so the cat feels the same.
However, it is not always the same place that he wants
for himself; he changes his mind from time to time. He
will sit in a particular chair constantly and for months
you will have difficulty in removing him. One day, for
no evident reason he will desert it and find another
corner.

His bed   He is entitled to his special place and it should be fur-
nished to his liking. Usually, this is where you will put

his box or basket. A basket is fiddly to clean if any dirt or wetness gets onto it and, when it loses its freshness, begins to look dowdy. I recommend a moderately roomy box that can be replaced with a similar one at any time. It should be about fifteen inches long and ten inches wide and about eight inches high – not too big, for big boxes are less cosy. It should be warm and draught-proof.

Line the base with newspaper for cats love to sit on them, possibly because they get warm quickly. Use a whole folded newspaper, for the cat will claw the layers to soften them. Over this you can lay his own cloth, a towel, a blanket or a shawl. Keep a couple of such blankets ready and clean for his box but change them only when they are dirty. If you change them too often, you will destroy the cosiness which he has made for himself and he will 'go off' the box and stop using it. It does not matter if there is a little dust in the corners, for you will be clearing it away in a day or two, before it has time to breed germs.

If you suspect he is harbouring fleas, sprinkle the bottom of the box, especially under the blanket, with a little anti-pest powder. You could do this regularly as a safeguard.

You will find that a loving cat will want to sit on your clothes when you put them down. He will pad up and down on a pullover or skirt, then settle down to purr on it. This is useful for, when you have discarded the garment, you can use it to line his box. It will make him very happy for he will have your scent around him all the time.

Though I have advised letting him choose where he wants his box you will have to be sensible about this. He may want to settle somewhere unsuitable, like inside an airing cupboard. He should be firmly discouraged from going into lockable cupboards at any time for he might be shut in for a day or more, unable to reach his food or his litter box.

If he does not want to go into his new box, do not force him. Just put it where he wants to go, with his blanket inside it, then ignore him. He will satisfy his curiosity and, if he likes it, he will settle down.

In addition to a bed he will require several items of toiletry, at least a brush and, possibly, a comb.

His food Have a supply of at least half-a-dozen small dishes for his food. If you keep the same dish for the same kind of food, he will learn in time that fish comes in a square tin, canned food in a saucer, milk in a round dish, or something like that. Then he will show you which food he prefers as soon as he sees which dish you have picked up. When he is hungry or thirsty he will sniff at the appropriate dish to show what he wants. Having a number of dishes also makes it easier for you to keep his dishes absolutely clean. There should be no quick rinse off with the old food scraps to make room for the next meal; that makes the dishes smell stale and makes the cat reject his food. Let the dishes soak for a while before washing them.

You would be wise never to put food into his sleeping box or basket for, if food is spilled, it will make a mess and the bedding will smell. Put it near enough to his box for him to smell it but out of the way of passing feet.

Playthings   For all cats, especially young ones, you will need playthings. He will regard many of the objects around him as toys, such as the brush and the towel and anything that swings within his reach. He will play with a ring that is left near him, or with a pen or a typewriter ribbon and will bite magazines at the corners. He is not being mischievous when he does these things. It is natural for him to play with everything that attracts him but he will be less interested in your things if he has enough of his own playthings around him. Walnuts and ping-pong balls make a lovely noise and he can never catch them. Something dangling just within reach – or just beyond reach – will give him a lot of exercise as well as fun. A small soft toy that he can ravage with his teeth will engage his attention; if it is a little floppy he will think it is fighting him back and he will enjoy that. It should be small enough to carry but not small enough to go right into his mouth.

His litter box   Finally, if he is very young, or if he lives in a flat, you will need a litter box. Do *not* use a cardboard or wooden box, but one that can be washed out; a metal or plastic one will not absorb moisture. It should be about twelve to fifteen inches square and about three inches deep, big enough for him to sit right inside and stretch out his tail. Half-fill the box with soil, or some brand of cat litter, or even sawdust. In an emergency wood shavings or torn bits of newspaper would do. Place it out of the way, preferably under a piece of furniture, for he prefers to be private and protected. When he is at his toilet an animal wants to hide, as he is vulnerable to attack from possible enemies.

Outside cattery   You may intend to own a number of cats, not only as pets but for breeding or showing. You will not want them all to live in your house so you will need an outside cattery. Unless the conditions of the terrain where the cattery will stand are known, little advice can be given about this except in general terms.

   Since such cats will have to be kept apart from strays and unwelcome marauders, you will have to provide a closed cage, probably constructed from wood and wire-

An outside cattery will be necessary if you intend to own a number of cats, whether for breeding or showing

netting. Two sections are required; one for the cats to rest and sleep in warmth and quiet, the other for them to play and take exercise. Separate cubicles can be made for each cat, or a communal cage for all. In the latter case several beds should be provided, for the cats may want to sleep apart. The beds or cubicles should be off the ground, lined with something warm and cosy, and with free access to the food and exercise section. Small-mesh wire-netting will keep out other small animals which would steal the cats' food. Presumably you will want to control the mating, so a partition will be needed to separate the sexes. Or, make separate cages, not near each other.

To be able to go into the cages without letting the cats out, will necessitate some kind of double door – a short passage with a door at each end, like the barbican of an ancient castle.

Low level heating may be needed in cold weather but neither too hot, nor too concentrated. Of course, the top should be rainproof as well as catproof, for nothing distresses a cat more than a cold wet bed. Outside lighting should be provided, too, for you will sometimes need to go into the cabins after dark. If you are very fussy about the conditions of your cats you can provide a separate cabin for each animal, though it is not really necessary. If traps are built into the sides of the cabins, food can be placed in the cabins from the outside.

Teaching your cat

One of the pleasures of having pets is teaching them to be happy and healthy animals. It is fascinating to watch as your kitten develops its natural skills and laps and eats, runs, jumps and climbs but it is more fun as it learns how to keep itself clean, how to wait for its food, how to understand you and which chairs and rooms it may or may not use. A lot of patience is essential and you must be prepared to teach the same thing over and over again, until it really understands that you intend to be obeyed.

Habits Do not let any bad habits even begin to form, for cats are unbelievably conservative. Once they do something in a certain place or in a certain way they will want to repeat it in the same place and in the same way. For instance, if it follows you down the stairs it will pass you, or wait for you, on exactly the same stair every time, no matter how fast or slowly you go. You can use this characteristic by showing him how to behave properly. The earlier you start, the easier it will be for, although you may teach a kitten a lot of things and an older cat some things, it is difficult to make it forget something it has learned on its own.

A cat is a wilful creature and if you try to persuade it against its inclination, it will run away. You may be able to teach it *NOT* to do something more easily than to *DO* anything. It may learn not to go into certain rooms, cupboards or boxes, or onto a particular chair, by reproaching it when it does so but it will be more difficult to teach it to use the chair you have chosen for it, unless it wants to do so.

Feeding If you decide that your cat must eat in a special corner then, of course, you must always put the feeding bowl there, and never feed the cat anywhere else. If you do and the cat prefers the alternative place it will wait there and miaow for a long time at each feed. A cat is a great optimist and is convinced that you will relent and let it have its own way. It may carry its food to the place it prefers so you must be ready to carry it back.

The same treatment goes for its sleeping place and, especially, for toilet training. Make sure that the place you have chosen is not cold or draughty and has no unpleasant odour, then be quite adamant.

Teaching a kitten Start teaching the kitten as soon as it begins to find its way round the house. Immediately it tries to go into a forbidden place, such as the airing cupboard, make a sharp noise. I usually hiss and that 'psssst' sound stops the kitten in its tracks, but you could clap your hands or say 'booh' or 'no'. If the kitten still tries to get into the cupboard, repeat the noise and, perhaps, hold the kitten firmly, until it understands.

Punishment The question of punishment must come up sooner or later. Your cat may be punished only at the second it is caught misbehaving; not later on, for then it will see no connection. Whatever you do, there must be love in your heart so that the cat will not feel that it has lost your affection. A smart slap on the rump, accompanied by a sharp word, is quite adequate. Never hit it with a stick unless you are trying to make it afraid of sticks. Then you would only need to wiggle it to stop the cat misbehaving. Probably the cat would simply run away without learning much. I find that 'psssst' is efficient enough.

How can you teach it not to jump onto the table? Sweep it off very firmly and definitely every time you see it there. Make sure nothing inviting is left on the table, such as open food or milk. Put all the cat's food in the proper place and be consistent. Do not allow it to go there sometimes; the cat must learn that it is NEVER allowed on the table.

Clawing and scratching You will find it difficult to stop your cat clawing at upholstered furniture if it once starts, so fix a scratching post near where it plays or sleeps and let it get used to that by scraping its paws on it from time to time. Meanwhile keep it out of the rooms where there is fabric-covered furniture. A scratching post is simply a

29

stout stick with a bit of old carpet or canvas round it. Later, it may scratch the wood itself.

Most cats like to claw and scratch although the reason is not fully understood. It seems to be a way of stretching the tendons and strengthening the claws. It must do this somewhere, and the backs of chairs are so tempting. You will often find bits of shell from the claw-tips on the floor near-by. If your cat lives an indoor life he may need to have his claws clipped by a vet occasionally. Outdoor cats wear down their claws naturally.

Toilet training

One of the first things you will want to teach your kitten is to use its litter box or tray (see Chapter 2). Of course, the kitten will prefer to go outside so it should have access to a yard or garden as early as possible. Make a flap door, or leave a window open with a stool near-by to help it up until it can jump to the sill. However, until it can go out at will, it must have its tray.

Start training even before it leaves the maternity box by carrying it to the tray from time to time and touching the soil with its paw, especially after its mother has used it. If it has no mother at home, try to put a little of its own excreta in the box as soon as possible.

Should the kitten make a mistake and drop a puddle in the wrong place clean it up at once and disinfect the spot to remove the smell. If the smell remains, the kitten will return again and again. If you actually see the kitten messing in the wrong place sweep it off its feet immediately – make a fuss, stamp on the floor, hiss or do what you like to startle it. If it persists, you can smack it a little. It will learn in time.

Cleaning

Finally, there is the question of cleaning itself. This should be perfectly natural to the kitten from about six or eight weeks and it should do so regularly after a meal, or when it is resting. It may need some help, especially if it is a long-haired variety. It will certainly keep itself cleaner if you show that you are interested. Daily brushing would be ideal but this takes time. The cat will love it and will purr loudly throughout. Do this as often as you can, with an occasional combing to get rid of the tangles and hard bits of dirt. Use talcum powder very sparingly and brush out well after application.

If the cat gets lazy you can try putting cream or butter on the dirty parts but these are not recommended, for butter picks up dirt easily. Just keep your pet happy and healthy, show that you care about its being clean, and you should have no serious difficulty.

No tricks *Note* that I have not suggested you should try to teach your cat tricks of any kind. You are expecting too much if you try to teach it some unnatural activity which would cause it to lose much of its dignity. Any feats of jumping and climbing which it wants to do will be natural to its development and when it has learned enough from any activity, it will give up.

Feeding Your cat will tell you more about its food than books can, though you should take his advice grudgingly. He will demand only the best and ignore anything he is not used to, unless you keep firm control.

All cats have their feeding quirks and whims, just like people. They get a fixed idea of what they want and, if you let them have too much of their own choice, you will have difficulty in changing them to other forms of feeding.

Fish Most cats like fish. A fishmonger has many off-cuts, usually called 'pieces', which vary from day to day and are very cheap. There is no reason why your pet should not rely entirely on these for all his fish requirements. Occasionally you can buy unsmoked haddocks or whitings and boil them whole; or pieces of coley, which has no bones. All my cats have eaten these fish, including some of the bones, with no difficulty at all, separating uneatable bones with ease. Do not give herrings with small slender bones; these are not easy to avoid and may get stuck in the cat's mouth or stomach. Many books advise sorting out all bones before giving fish to cats. My experience has been that they are quite capable of doing this themselves and seem to enjoy crunching smaller bones, apart from the herring.

Meat Raw meat is also a part of a cat's natural diet. Raw minced beef, occasionally tiny pieces of liver or other meat, can only do good. Do not be concerned if some small pieces are swallowed whole for the cat will digest them.

Cooked meat is also useful and keeps fresh longer than raw meat. All canned food is pre-cooked and is an obvious easy option, for it facilitates your task considerably. However, canned food should be used sparingly, not exclusively. Kitchen scraps are another equally useful way of feeding. Puss will soon show you his preference.

Other 'likes' Many cats love vegetables and some even like spicy foods. They eat flour-foods, too, and love cakes, bread and butter, and some cereals. Very few cats eat fruit. Some will eat grass and it is said to help their digestion. They even nibble flowers. It is a good policy to make sure that a town cat has access to grass or other greenery in a garden or park; otherwise, fresh cut coarse grass can be brought home for him. I have heard of only one wholly vegetarian cat.

Dry foods Among the prepared pet foods is a growing number which resembles hard cereals. They are of different flavours, and presumably contents, and are similar to the tinned foods. As they are dry they do not attract flies and can be left in the dish for a longer time. My cats have loved some of these dry foods and it is interesting to hear them crunching the hard bits.

How much food? This varies from day to day, from one cat to another, from mood to mood; it also depends on the food offered. I find that an adult cat will eat from half a pound to one pound of fish in a day, put down in two meals. Feed him twice daily, the second time late at night to ensure he comes home then. Kittens require rather less feed per day and they take it more often, in smaller portions. Feed a kitten four times daily, giving it only as much as it will finish at once. Tinned foods are not of equal value nor equally appetising. Two tins daily are needed for a cat, less for a kitten.

When a cat rubs against your leg obviously pleading for food, it shows that either the quality or quantity of its food is not up to standard. Do not be too disappointed if a good deal of your cat's affection seems to start in its tummy and as soon as you feed it, the loving stops, only to return when it is next hungry.

Cats sometimes eat and drink very odd things, such as berries, leaves, tomato juice, apple tart, tree bark.

Drinking Books normally recommend that you should put out clean cold tap-water for cats to drink, in addition to milk. I have never seen a cat drink tap-water unless it was dripping from the tap – and that was partly a game, I believe. Bowls of clean water were put out for years until I noticed that they would drink almost any other kind of water – that in the fish tank, the washing-up bowl, the sink – in preference.

Occasionally, treat your pet to milk top or cream. Then he will drink his fill but you should regard this as a food, not a drink.

Fasting Never leave a kitten for a long time without food. An adult cat may be left for a whole day without food without coming to any harm – indeed, an over-weight cat will benefit from an occasional fast. However, if you have left a cat for a whole day without food *DO NOT* give him a very large feed immediately, for he will simply gorge the lot, then go away and be sick and be just as hungry as if he had not eaten.

Long-haired whites about 4 weeks old

Breeds

Differences between breeds Without being too emphatic, while it is true that some breeds of cats have qualities of character which make them just a little different from other breeds, all breeds share many basic qualities.

For instance, Siamese tend to be more communicative in an obvious way; short-haired cats can keep themselves clean more easily than long-haired. Certain cats enjoy swimming but then, most can do so – though it is rarely necessary. They keep out of water instinctively, for it clogs their fur and they cannot shake themselves free of it as dogs do. Do not try to make your cat swim, for it will probably hate it and, staying wet, might catch cold.

Obviously, long-haired cats climb through hedges and up trees less often than short-haired ones, for they realise their fur will hamper them.

An elderly Siamese (this one is sealpoint) can be as sedate as any other breed

Siamese cats, especially when very young, seem to be more interested in human beings and their affairs than other breeds. They also react to voices more readily and they are more easily taught to be obedient, to scratch their special posts, use a toilet tray, even walk on a lead. Siamese are considered to be the intellectuals of the cat fraternity. This has as much to do with their appearance as their behaviour, for other breeds are often just as intelligent. An old Siamese is usually just as sedentary and dull as any other breed of cat, while a neutered Siamese shows all the same characteristics as other cats. It is a fallacy that Siamese cats are vicious for they are just as docile and friendly as their owners make them, as are all other cats.

Siamese, Burmese and Abyssinian breeds are similar in their attention to voices. I have held 'conversations' with several – i.e. a certain word or sound from me brought the response of a specific sound from the cat. On the other hand, I have owned mongrel cats who knew several words including *No, Out, Down, In* and *Come in.*

As your cat develops its own special characteristics he will seem to be a breed all his own!

Colour and character
It is very unlikely that colour has anything to do with character, although certain cats, usually the *long-haired, blue-eyed whites,* are deaf. A lady who lived in South London believed that the lack of pigmentation

had something to do with it so, by selective breeding with cats whose eyes were slightly coloured, she succeeded in producing a series of litters of kittens which had perfect hearing. Whether the colour, or lack of it, was the deciding factor cannot be proved at the moment, but the kittens were very good evidence. Similar cats with even a few coloured hairs are not deaf.

If you do own a deaf kitten, do not be worried about him for he will be a very good pet if you take his deafness into consideration.

The *ginger tom*, which should be called the *red tabby*, has a reputation for being a fighter, probably because of its colour. It has a tendency to roam and may grow very large when neutered. Ginger toms are more violent and ruthless fighters even as kittens, besides being slightly more nervous. The *ordinary tabby*, grey or gold, has always seemed to me to be the happiest and most playful kitten in my litters. In my experience it has been an indisputable fact that the simple tabby has learned more quickly than other kittens in the same litter. It has been the first to climb out of the 'nursery' box, the first to play with my hand, the first to fight in fun and the first to climb onto my lap to settle down. For this I have no explanation.

Ginger tom or Red tabby

In contrast, the *black-and-white kittens* have been almost always the last to emerge and the last to make friends with strangers. They have been even more timid than the red tabbies.

Similarities One characteristic is common to all breeds; they are very selfish creatures. They may like to please you but will take little trouble to do so. They are mean to each other, even to their own kittens after the first few weeks. If there is only a little food in sight they will fight forward to have it, even though they can see that there is more to come. They do not think of the future – they want food NOW and will not let you rest until they have it.

Cats of all breeds are curious. They will put their noses to everything new that comes near to them and will sniff anything you put on the floor or climb into any box, bag or basket you leave open. They will not

Sealpoint Siamese

only look at a stranger but, if they are friendly cats, they will jump onto his lap to examine him more closely. So they should. If a cat does not do this, it is either too timid or has a poor sense of smell. They will touch almost any small object with a paw to see if it moves, unless they are afraid of it.

It is important to treat a cat gently until it has enough courage to give way to its natural curiosity. This is the cat's natural way of distinguishing between eatable and uneatable, between friend and foe.

Mousers Good cats of all breeds make good mousers. They are not hunting the mouse for prey any more; they are chasing an object that has excited them. The fact that cats play 'cat and mouse' games with small animals like mice shows that they are not chasing them for food. They will just as happily chase an inanimate object like a bit of fur or a toy mouse, knowing it is not alive. It is fun. Your cat might even pick up a mouse very gently, then put it down to watch it run around.

If, however, it kills the mouse and gets the taste in its mouth then, probably, the mouse will be eaten. Personally, I do not think the killing is the main object of the chase. Some people believe that a hungry cat will chase mice more readily than a well-fed one but since they do not hunt for food, this cannot be true. A healthy, well cared for cat will chase anything that moves, including mice. An over-fed cat will chase nothing, not even mice. So if you have acquired a pet cat simply as a sort of mouse-trap feed it normally, keep it fit and let it roam at will. The smell of the cat will keep most mice at bay.

It is also a fallacy that cats are self-sufficient. They are no longer independent of humans and should not be left alone to fend for themselves for long periods. It is an offence to leave a cat without attendance even for a few days.

Strays

Stray cats are not living independent lives. They are nearly all badly fed, unclean and full of vices. They search for food in human habitations and live off bad food in dustbins and rubbish heaps, although many people find strays and leave food out for them. They rarely live well or long without help from people. Some strays live in derelict houses and factories. Mistakenly, some soft-hearted people feed them instead of calling in one of the animal rescue societies. Thus, the cats settle in as permanent strays, breed and rear families, and the situation gets worse. Stray cats nearly always turn into rogue cats, stealing into houses to feed from the bowls of pet cats and the larders where pets do not go. They carry diseases and pests around with them and frequently die in misery.

Breed standards

Breeds are officially named according to a set of standards laid down by the Governing Council of the Cat Fancy. New breeds are being created every few years, though the variations are now little more than slight changes in colour, sometimes in head or body shape. General body shape for various breeds is also described by the Governing Council. There are thirty-three named breeds, plus sub-classes up to a total of about sixty.

Long-haired white
(Persian)

Long hair   Officially, there are three lengths of hair – long, medium and short. Among the long-haired breeds are the Persians and Chinchillas. They have a lot of fluffy hair which sticks out almost straight from the body in most parts. It should not be smoothed down.

Short hair   These cats should be sleek, smooth and shiny, especially if they are Siamese, Burmese, Abyssinian, Havana or Russian – or even the mixed-breed ordinary witch's black cat.

Medium hair   This is a less common breed, the British Blue being a good example. The cat on page 85 of this book has medium-length hair. These cats are sometimes referred to as 'rough-coated'.

Colours   These are so numerous that little purpose would be served by listing them. New colours appear and new combinations of patches for colouration are approved from time to time. Self-colour means the same colour all over. Colour-point means that the cat has, usually, a white body with a colour on certain specified places: these are the four paws, the tail-end, the ears and the mask or face. The main colours are red (which is ginger), blue (which is a kind of bluey-grey), brown and black. Siamese sometimes come in a further variety of shades such as lilac, chocolate and tabby points. The favourite colour which is almost exclusive to Siamese is sealpoint – a rich deep brown, very beautiful indeed.

Purists specify exactly how much of each point is to be coloured although the colour of the points spreads over the whole body as the cat ages.

Tabbies can be either fine or rough. Fine tabbies have many slender lines all across their bodies and round their legs and tails. They are usually slightly heavier than other tabbies. Rough tabbies are more common and have a definite pattern of black stripes and shapes

Tabby point Siamese

Bluepoint Siamese

Cornish Rex

'Myki' – torty & white

on various parts of the body. There is a sort of letter M above the eyes, a sideways letter V on each cheek, a stripe down the spine and a round patch in the middle of each side. The base colour can be gold or silver and they normally have white underparts. They can have any length of hair. In certain lights you will find tabby markings on many cats that are not supposed to be tabbies, especially if you smooth down sleek short fur.

Tortoiseshell cats have a fairly even mixture of ginger and black hair all over, even underneath. By official decision these colours should be in small even patches, not brindled (or speckled), although one of my best and most beautiful cats was brindled.

Tortoiseshell and white cats are unlike the tortoiseshell in that the patches can be much bigger and need not be in any pattern. They usually have white underparts and, officially, should have no white above, and should show no tabby markings. However, my best cat of all was not evenly marked and had clear tabby marks in her ginger patches.

a   *b*

c   *d*

a   Red tabby
b   Red Abyssinian
c   Blue Burmese
d   Havana
e   Long-haired red-self

e

Manx

Manx cats are of two kinds but for shows only one kind is recognised. They are called the rumpy and the stumpy. Rumpies have no sign of a tail at all, though a slight bump can sometimes be felt where a tail might have been. Even this slight bump is not officially tolerated. The stumpy has a more prominent protuberance, perhaps an inch or two. They can be of any colour and any hair length. There are also Manx cats *with* tails.

Albino cats are pure white all over and their eyes are very pale, perhaps a pinkish blue. They can be of any hair length.

Rex cats have very curly or wavy hair which is rather hard to the touch, and can be any colour, though most are self-colour brown, black, or red. There is little difference between Cornish Rex and Devon Rex. Either might be almost whiskerless; any whiskers they have are usually very short and curly, as if singed.

The Rex quality of hair is being bred into other cats and a Siamese cat with wavy hair is called a Si-Rex. A normal Rex cat is nowadays being bred to type and a standard for head and body shape is being established.

Van cats, said to originate from Turkey, are mostly colour points. These are cats most familiarly known to swim easily and naturally. Most of those I have seen have medium-length hair.

Showing   If you feel your cat has a good pedigree and might be suitable for showing in Breed Classes or Breed Shows, you should write to the Governing Council of the Cat Fancy for their list of standards, the price being 20p. The address of the Secretary is: Mrs W. Davis, Dovefields, Petworth Road, Witley, Surrey.

Most shows have classes for pet cats – indeed some local shows are solely for pets. A pet cat must be extremely well cared for to reach the standards set for good class shows, so go along to see one of the shows before putting your cat forward.

Albino Siamese

Judging Blue Persians

In the annual Championship Show of the National Cat Club in Olympia, London, there is even a class for rescued cats, that is for cats which were strays and were given a home and brought up to show standard.

No matter what colour or breed or class of cat you own, if it is a pet and treated properly it will be just as loving and lovable as any pedigree cat.

Holidays

There is no reason why your cat should not go with you on holiday. Many boarding-houses will accept pets, either in outside accommodation, or in your room. Write to ask permission first, of course. Look for details in holiday guide books – especially in *Pets Welcome*. If your cat is regarded as part of the family it is natural that you would want to take it with you.

If the place is suitable, you should have no difficulty with the cat itself, so long as it is used to going on outings with you.

Taking the cat out

From the time it is a kitten you should take it out with you – on a visit to friends, for walks in the woods, to follow you through the fields, to sit with you on the beach. Why not? You could get it used to a lead if you wished but that is not necessary and can be a hindrance if a dog begins to chase it. Start taking the kitten out while still very young and let it run about in the grass or in a strange house, keeping it in sight. After a few outings, it will be used to the idea and, though it may wander off quite a long way, it will follow you as you move along. My own system was not to feed the cat very much, but let it see that I had food with me. It kept fairly near to me in order to be there when food was put out.

My cats, Pinkie and Too-too, climbed trees in Epping Forest, ran along logs, snuggled in long grass, or simply sat by my side. They sometimes followed at a distance of fifty yards if I walked away. As soon as I approached the car, which they knew very well, they caught up with me and jumped in without hesitation.

Camping

Some friends of mine have had several cats all of which have been taken camping many times. Suzi and Twinks meandered around other tents on the sites, making friends with other campers. On the journey the children look after the cats, even for hundreds of miles.

Car travel   It is dangerous to travel alone in a car with a loose cat
for it may have a sudden desire to sit on the driver's lap
or shoulder, with a tail waving before his eyes, while a
kitten might play among the pedals. If you must travel
alone with a cat put it into a basket, preferably one
with a wire door so that it can see you, and where you
can put an affectionate finger through the bars to fondle
it. Do not travel too far before letting it out to find a
toilet. The cat may be a little car-sick on the first few
journeys but it soon gets over this.

There may be times when you have to leave it in a
car for some time and, of course, a window should be
left slightly open for ventilation. Make sure this gap is
tiny, for cats can squeeze through incredibly small
spaces. Do not park the car in the sun for it can become
unbearably hot inside. Leave a little milk or water in a
bowl. Make sure the cat does not need a toilet. Do not
leave it for a long time, or it will become very distressed, thinking itself abandoned and imprisoned.

I have heard of wire guards for car windows which
enable the windows to be left open, the cat safe and
comfortable and the car still burglar-proof.

Boarding-houses   If you are taking your cat to a boarding-house with you take as much of its own belongings as you conveniently can: the box and the towel on which it sleeps, its feeding bowls, a supply of its usual food and its litter tray. Every cat that travels should be used to a litter tray. Before letting it loose in strange surroundings, ask the permission of the boarding-house owner, who will know of any hazards, especially other cats or un-friendly dogs.

Leaving it at home   If you do not intend to take your cat with you, try to arrange for it to be looked after in the house of a well-known friend. As a poor alternative ask a friend to visit your home at least once a day to feed your cat and, possibly, clean up any mess. The cat should be able to go out and find company when it pleases. If this is not possible it must be sent to a good boarding cattery. It must not be left to fend for itself.

   Cattery charges vary between 25p and 60p per day, according to the standard, the locality and the facilities. Some cattery owners arrange to collect the cat in a basket, either from its home, or from a station if it is sent by train. This means a small extra charge.

Communal cattery   There are two types of boarding catteries. If your cat has been neutered, it can go to a communal type of

A communal type of boarding cattery   *An individual cabin*

cattery, where all the cats live together in a kind of open cage. They have separate bed boxes and plenty of space to roam around for exercise. This is definitely the best for many cats.

Separate cabins The other type of cattery has a separate cage, called a cabin, for each cat. The cats are let out in turn into a larger cage for daily exercise, under supervision. The people who run these places will look after your pet very well, for they are all animal lovers. They sometimes sit with the cats, or go into the cages to talk and play with them. In any case, all these establishments have to be licensed and are open to inspection. A pregnant cat should never be left, for she becomes apprehensive and dependent on you at this time. I know of premature and still-births which have resulted from doing so. If you cannot take her with you then a friend's help should be found.

In boarding catteries the risk of infection from other cats is very slight, for the precautions taken are strict. On your part you must make sure that your cat is healthy and free from pests. It would be unfair to put

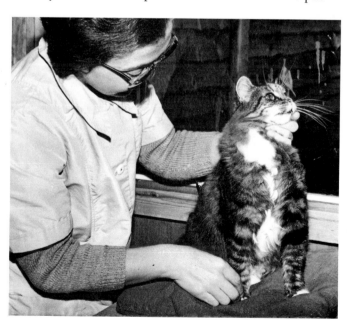

A cat being inspected before admittance to a boarding cattery

at risk all the other boarders in the cattery and, at the same time, ruin the reputation of the cattery.

One excellent boarding cattery with seventy cabins near Windsor has very strict rules for the health of its charges. Males must have been neutered. Each cat must have had full doses of anti-infection treatment, including a booster not less than three weeks before the holiday and must not have visited a vet or a show, during the preceding three weeks. On arrival, every cat is inspected in a separate room before being admitted. If a vet is called in to a cat (for which the owner would have to pay) he treats the cat in a special isolated cabin.

You could not take such good care of the cat yourself!

Mating, birth and neutering

One of the happiest times for you with a pet cat comes when she is producing and nursing her own kittens, in your home. It is also a time of extra trouble for you, though it is well worth while, especially if you have arranged the mating yourself.

Pedigree cats If she is a pedigree cat and you want to produce pedigree kittens, you will have to watch her constantly, so that she will not get out and mate haphazardly with unknown cats. You will need to keep her indoors from the age of seven months and, as you cannot be sure when she will come 'into season', she will have to be kept indoors *all* the time. 'In season' is the expression used for the several times in the year when a female cat is most anxious to find a mate and have sexual relations with him.

'In season' She shows this by her behaviour. She howls a little (especially if she is Siamese, which can moan and howl both loudly and often) and she rolls about on the floor, squirms on your lap, rubs her muzzle against your face, almost whimpering at times. When she sees a possible mate, even through a window, she becomes even more

A female cat 'in season'

53

agitated, rolling over and waving her paws, stretching her legs, pawing and clawing in the air.

Mating If you decide to mate her with another pedigree cat you should have made previous arrangements with a good breeder who has a stud available. When your 'queen' – that is, a female cat of breeding age – comes into season you telephone the owner of the stud male and arrange to take your cat to him the same or next day. You can obtain lists of breeders with cats at stud from the Governing Council of the Cat Fancy, from various cat societies, and from advertisements in show catalogues and pet magazines. The owner of the stud cat will see that the right male is put with your queen, and may even help the actual mating process. Then, in a day or two, your queen will be ready for collection. This usually costs from three to ten guineas, according to the status of the male in the cat world, especially in shows and as a stud cat.

Mating away from home If, on the other hand, your cat is an ordinary pet female and finds her own mates, you may find that she shows less of these 'in season' signs at home, keeping them for display to the male when she finds him out of doors.

When she mates she may stay away from home for one or two nights, even longer. A virulent male will sometimes 'imprison' his females by some form of masterful behaviour, holding her by his side in the grass or under a hedge, mating with her several times before releasing her.

Males Males do not have seasons in the same way as females so they are ready to mate most of the time and, when a

Mating

female comes to him 'in season', he takes the opportunities she offers. While she is held by him she may not eat for a day or two. When she does come home she will be ready for a good meal.

During the actual mating, if you have not seen it happen before, you may feel that he is attacking her savagely, but this is not so. Do not interfere. He will seize her firmly by the back of the neck, and pull her head down or back. He mounts onto her back, straddling her rear parts. She may squeal a little, but will not struggle to get away. After a few minutes, when he has finished and released her, she is usually in a highly excited condition. She rolls over and over, yelping and squealing, squirming and wriggling in ecstasy. After a few minutes, during which he may sit and watch her in amazement, he may repeat the whole process. If he is an older or more experienced cat he will possibly hold her near to him for an hour or two, until he is ready for more mating. This procedure will take place several times in one day. Both cats quieten down in a day or two and, eventually either he releases her, or she decides that she has had enough, and escapes.

More than one male may mate with a queen in this way in one season. Once she is pregnant, however, she will not want to take another mate and fights off any unwelcome attentions.

Gestation The gestation period (sixty-three days is normal) is a pleasant time, for your cat will become closer to you as time goes by. She begins to put on weight after about two weeks and by six or seven weeks has reached full size. At this point it is interesting to see the kittens

A pregnant cat

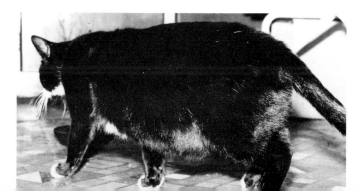

moving about, especially when the mother lies on her side. During this period of nine weeks she will stay at home rather more, for she cannot climb so easily, or jump, or squeeze through the usual restricted spaces, and she knows she is more vulnerable if she meets an adversary. She may eat a little more, but not much, and she will probably drink more. There is no need to vary her diet. Keep her comfortable and show her that you understand what is happening to her.

The maternity ward Your cat will require a deep box in a dark place, plenty of warmth and softness, and privacy. She will begin to look for this hideaway about a week before the kittens are due to arrive, so make sure you provide the right accommodation. As soon as she begins to peer into corners and lie in the dark you should put out a number of boxes, lining them with the cat's own blankets. When she finally chooses one, line it with an old disposable blanket. I have tried out many kinds of boxes for a 'maternity ward' and have found that an egg box cut and tied as in the photograph is ideal. It can be laid on its back or stood on its side, with the door either at the top or bottom. The cats have always been happy with them.

With the box on its back, the side provides a sort of shelf where the mother can sit and watch her kittens, just out of their reach. She will sometimes sit there with her tail down inside the box for the kittens to play with.

The box must be deep enough to keep the young kittens inside warm and out of draughts but easy for the mother to get in and out at will. When the kittens are capable of climbing out of the box, they will be qualified to be allowed to move around the house, strong enough and lively enough and, what is more important, interested enough to get out and explore.

Birth of the kittens Most cats give birth with no trouble at all. One day a cat will go into its box and, before you know what is happening, there will be several tiny bodies, all licked clean and dried off, lying under her, feeding from the right places, and she will be purring happily with eyes half closed, completely contented.

Unless she is used to having kittens, do not try to watch them being born. She is wondering what on earth is happening to her, and trying to cope with the wet and struggling bundles that are emerging from her hind quarters, licking them, and holding them close, one by one. She cannot cope with entertaining you at the same time. If you know that the kittens have started to appear, stay around so that she can feel you near if she needs you. If nothing is wrong, she will be much happier managing alone. Normally, only a sick or stupid cat will need help but if there is some complication any cat may need help. In this case, call the vet at once and do not try to do anything yourself. Perhaps the cat may not be able to sever the umbilical cord, or a kitten may not come out easily. If any kittens are born dead the mother will push them to one side. As soon as possible put a hand into the box, make sure she is not lying on a kitten, and remove any still-born. Do nothing else for an hour or two, then put a large bowl of milk near to her. She could drink up to half a pint before going back to the kittens.

She should lick them all clean at once, and they will dry in a few minutes. She will put them to feed from her almost immediately, and they will go to the right place either by smell or instinct, straight to a nipple which has been forming for several days, and is now the right size and shape. The kittens will fight for a place to feed, even at this early stage, but there will be enough places, even for quite a large family. One of my cats, Too-too, eventually had eleven teats, though not all in use at the same time. The average size of a litter is four or five. Up to a dozen have been known for one litter, but this is rare.

The kittens Within a day or two of birth, inspect every kitten and make a thorough examination to ensure that each one is healthy and complete. Tell your vet if there is any sign of disease, runny nose or eyes, sores or deformities. The vet will probably advise you to have any that are not fit enough to be reared or are deformed put to sleep and it is wise to take his advice.

Leave the family in the same box for a day or two,

then remove all the soiled bedding. Put a little pest powder between the folds and underneath the clean blankets.

As soon as you have decided whether to keep any of the kittens yourself, find homes for the rest. Invite the future owners to see their kittens and get to know them from about two weeks old.

You need do nothing to help the mother rear the kittens for the first weeks. Just watch them grow and see how they learn to cope with life. Note how they develop differently; how, right from the first days, one of them becomes a bully and one the underdog; how loudly they purr – more loudly than their mother does. For a fortnight do nothing except let them get used to the smell and feel of your hand as you stroke each one for a few seconds a day. When they begin to move about and to recognise and welcome you, about a week later, you may take them out and play with them in a warm room, very gently, but only for a few minutes at a time. At about six weeks they will emerge from the box themselves, and that is when you will be able to enjoy the fun of playing with them, caring for them, feeding them, and generally bearing the responsibility for their lives until they go to their new homes.

Neutering If you do not intend to breed from your cat, it is advisable to have it 'doctored' or neutered. This means that females are spayed by having their ovaries removed and males are castrated by having their testicles removed. These are fairly simple operations for a vet and take only an hour or two. The cats suffer no serious immediate effects and recover quite quickly.

When to neuter? There are several opinions about the best time of life to have a cat neutered but medical opinion favours the fifth or sixth month, in any case before the male's first mating or the female's first litter; preferably before the first time a female comes 'into season'. Some people feel that females should be allowed one litter, males just one or two matings. You will have to make your own decision about this. The operation can be performed at a later age, but the younger the better. Whatever the age, of course, the cat must not be infected, pregnant, or 'in season' at the time. Cats that are not neutered are called 'whole' or 'entire' cats.

Effects Long-term effects vary and many cats seem to remain completely unaltered. A few show some physiological changes, still fewer show character changes. Any differences are understandable. Neutered males and females are no longer interested in each other sexually. Females do not come 'into season' so wandering males do not prowl round their houses. Males no longer spray their scent around to attract the attention of females, nor stay out for long periods looking for mates. Females, on the other hand, might wander out a little more for, as they do not attract the attentions of males, they are free to go as they please. Neutered cats are sometimes less active in other ways, which makes them rather fatter from lack of exercise. The males, particularly, often grow very large, even up to twice their normal weight and bulk.

Advantages There are two very important advantages of neutering. Far fewer unwanted kittens are born to stray female cats because of wandering males and owners have no problems either of protecting their females or of finding homes for unplanned kittens. In general, all the practical arguments are in favour of neutering pet cats, though you may have personal feelings against it. I have never had my cats neutered.

Common ailments

The signs of good health in a cat are clear and bright
eyes, a good appetite, activity and a lustrous coat. If
some of these are lacking, something is not quite right.
If your cat sits about listlessly, does not finish food
which he normally loves, lets his coat become dirty or
matted, shows the haws of his eyes for long periods, or
looks at you as if he is sorry for himself, you must
give him some attention. Perhaps he only needs attention, just some help with grooming, a little loving or a
change of food but it is important to watch for further
serious signs. If you see them, go to your vet at once.

Feline infectious gastro-enteritis is known to be a
killer disease. If you see a small pool of foamy froth or
vomit round the cat's mouth, and he is severely de-
pressed, immediate treatment is needed, for he could die
within twenty-four hours. This disease advances so
suddenly that people often feel that the cat has been
poisoned. Inoculation as a kitten can safeguard him.

Pawing his mouth, with much saliva can indicate
some obstruction, such as a small fish bone. If he will
let you, you could help him to remove it by using
tweezers or forceps. If not, hold his head firmly at the
back and squeeze the sides of his mouth while someone
else examines and removes the bone. It may be that the
cat has toothache or a loose tooth, or ulcerated gums or
throat. If he has *ulcers*, you will probably notice that
when he is hungry, he goes for his food, then withdraws
and refuses it. The vet will know whether a dental over-
haul or antibiotic treatment is required.

Constipation might be present when the cat tries to
excrete and strains hard. This can be relieved by dosing
him with medicinal liquid paraffin but it should not be
given over a long period. If he will not take the medicine in his food, you might have to hold him while you
administer it through the teeth at the side of his mouth.

Administering medicine by mouth

The same behaviour might indicate a *blocked bladder*; small stones obstruct the neck of the bladder and urethral tubes. Only the vet should deal with this situation.

Worms can be diagnosed by observing the cat. Since the worms eat most of his food before the cat benefits from it, he is always hungry and gets thinner. He may vomit and produce roundworms which are like small white earth-worms. In the faeces may be roundworms or tapeworms or even parts of tapeworms and you might see small bits of tapeworms, which look like dried rice, under the cat's tail, or in his toilet tray. The most effective treatment for this condition will be given by your vet who can write a prescription for a chemist to dispense, or you could buy some proprietary brand of medicine from a chemist or even a pet store.

Ringworm shows as a slight swelling with a tiny hard centre. As the area spreads, the hair round it disappears and the hard centre begins to ooze. This should be dealt with by your vet at once, as it is infectious. Do not let the cat wash itself there and do not touch it with your fingers. Ringworms are common just in front of the ears, where thinning of the hair is an early sign.

Sneezing and coughing may be a sign of cat 'flu or of catarrhal fever, if it persists for a time. In the case of either complaint there may be a discharge from eyes and nose and the cat will refuse food. Keep him warm in a draught-free room and take him to the vet as soon as possible.

Ear infections sometimes trouble cats at an early age. You may notice what appear to be pieces of dirt in your kitten's ears. On closer examination, particularly under a powerful magnifying glass, you would see that numerous mites had invaded them and the kitten will scratch his ears inside, even to the extent of making them bleed. Your vet will clean out the ears and give you an ointment or a dropper to deal with the infection.

Pills may be prescribed by your vet to administer to your cat and, as this is not easy at first, he will show you how to do it. Let the cat sit facing you, take his face in one hand, and squeeze his mouth. Have the pill ready at the finger-tips of the other hand. As your squeezing makes him open his mouth, quickly pop the pill right inside as far as you can, then hold his mouth closed. He will swallow the pill without difficulty and not even realise he has taken it. You can coat the pill with butter to help it to slip down.

Do not give aspirins to your cat. They can be fatal.

Powders can be sprinkled on foods, but this sometimes offends the cat's smell and he refuses the food. It is possible to administer powders in a way similar to that for pills, except that his head must be pulled back and the powder tipped down his throat – this is not quite so easy. Other medicines can sometimes be given with a syringe or mixed with milk. If your pet trusts you, he will not object to your unusual handling of him while you treat him.

If in any doubt do not treat the cat yourself, nor clean him up too much, for you might remove just those signs which the vet needs to see in order to help him diagnose the disease. Never give medicines that have been passed on to you by friends who think that their cat suffered the same complaint. They could be mistaken and, thus, kill your cat. All medicaments should be thrown away as soon as they are no longer needed. It is wrong to keep them, for they may not remain in good condition.

Deformities

a

a A cat with six toes
b 'Blind Jacob'
c A cat with an infected eye

Apart from the normal illnesses that afflict cats, sometimes things go wrong by accident. Among over 250 kittens produced in my home, several have been far from perfect. This has not always been so serious as it seemed at first. For instance, in a previous chapter I mentioned a crippled kitten which became a lovely pet. After that experience, another litter produced three kittens with their legs well out of shape. Instead of taking them to the vet to be put down, as I was advised, I treated them to a little course of gymnastics, moving their limbs in corrective exercises, and flicking them to make the kittens pay attention. Soon they began to move their own legs and, within a couple of weeks, the legs had a more normal shape. At the age of six weeks there was no difference between them and the other kittens. This was a successful experiment but I do not advise you to try it. However, a kitten should be given the chance to make a life for itself unless the vet advises against it. I once possessed an epileptic cat which was a beautiful and popular pet.

b   *c*

A cat in Kent has only three legs as the result of an accident on a farm. She is still a lively hunter and definitely a working farm cat, living a normal life.

A blind cat belonging to a friend of mine in Derbyshire is known as 'Blind Jacob'. His house is in a quarry at the side of a rocky cliff with wooded sides. He climbs the rocks, walks through the trees and returns home almost normally. His only real difficulties are knowing the height of a table or lap he wants to jump down from and keeping out of the way of his housemates, two healthy rushabout Staffordshire bull terriers.

These examples show that it is possible for a pet cat with physical shortcomings to live a happy and full life – with an understanding family of owners.

Orphans Sometimes a cat dies when bearing kittens. It happens also that a young cat either cannot or may not want to feed its kittens. You might overcome this by putting them gently to the teats once or twice and, perhaps, the new mother will tolerate it, even enjoy it. If she roughly struggles away, do not persist. She may have her reasons.

If she deserts them, the kittens will quickly die of cold on their own as their tiny bodies cannot keep themselves warm, so put a warm hot water bottle

A doll's feeding bottle makes a good substitute for a special fostering bottle

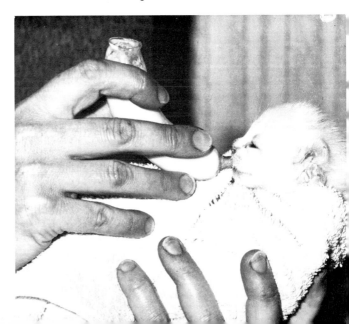

under the bedding and renew the water several times a day.

Then you face the task of feeding them many times a day for a week, less often for another two weeks, and less frequently for a further two weeks. You will also have to sponge them twice a day, dry them before a warm fire, and top-and-tail them twice a day. You will need a special fostering bottle, obtainable at a good pet shop, or a doll's feeding bottle and about two dozen teats, for the kittens will chew them. Alternatively, you can use a small syringe, such as those used by people for self-injection, but the teat should be tied onto this as the end is smooth and a kitten could swallow it. If teats are hard to find, try the specially shaped rubbers used in bicycle valves, after sterilising them. Syringes help kittens not used to sucking but do not press the syringe too much – you are not force feeding. A weak milky liquid, alternating with glucose or a sugar solution, finger warm, should be given with occasionally plain boiled water.

There are no strict rules for feeding, but the following routine might guide you.

Feed each kitten every two hours day and night, for about five days, giving each as much as it will take. Then lengthen the time to three hours and from the eighth or tenth day, miss out the least convenient feed. Strengthen the food gradually, adding a drop of cod liver oil or Brand's Essence or equivalent to some feeds. In the second week you could lengthen the times between the feeds; by the end of three weeks, you could supplement the diet with foods your vet recommends, or with baby foods. In the fourth week the kittens might feed from a spoon and learn to lap – if they do, most of your troubles are over. You will still need to sponge them daily and top-and-tail them frequently. They cannot do this for themselves.

Weaning can begin soon after the kittens learn to lap, and they may soon show an interest in such things as gravy, fish-water, even soft meat. At this stage you can congratulate yourself, for it is rare that orphan kittens pull through so far.

Development of hand-fed kittens is slower than

normal. They tend to be 'mini-kittens' and a little weaker for a few weeks. Later they should be normally healthy and active, though still smaller. It is also possible that they will lose some hair, or have diarrhoea until they are two or three months old.

It entails considerable sustained effort to rear motherless kittens and only if you are determined to go through with it have you the right to start. You must decide at their birth whether you want the kittens to survive. If not, you should ask your vet to put them down at once.

Pests All animals, including humans, harbour some kind of pest from time to time. Cats suffer from one or two kinds of pest, including ear mites and fleas, which are most common. In the ordinary way fleas are not harmful but are annoying because their bite causes an itch, and they carry some diseases.

A clean animal usually manages to keep itself fairly free of fleas and if you keep your cat healthy and happy it will never give you cause for concern. A miserable cat, however, which spends most of its time out of doors and in dirty surroundings, mixing with stray or unhealthy cats, picks up fleas very easily. Fleas can be detected by stroking a cat's fur against the natural lay, when specks of black deep down in the roots will show. They tend to group in warm spots, under the 'armpits' of forelegs and hind-legs, under the chin or round the neck. They hate to be exposed to light and fresh air. They move very quickly amongst the fur, so there is little likelihood of catching them. To get rid of them the whole cat must be treated.

Treatment First, sprinkle a large towel with any of the brands of pest powder suitable for cats (such as Pestroy or Vamoose) which contains pyrethrum or a similar chemical – this will be stated on the packet or tube.

Hold the cat firmly by the back of its neck and pour onto it more of the powder, rubbing well into the fur, deep down, backwards and forwards. Do not miss any small patches, even round the head, for the fleas will run from the powder and gather in any untreated places. Rub well between the legs, under the tail and along the tail with the towel round the cat. It will certainly protest, but keep the towel close round its neck and you will be able to hold it easily. The cat's eyes may water a little and will wash out any powder, though you should avoid the eyes. Then, without brushing the cat clean, turn it out in the garden, for the fleas will soon begin to jump off. It is a good idea to do the whole job out of doors, if possible. Hang the towel in the fresh air before you wash it. An hour or two later, when the cat has forgiven you for these indignities, give its fur a good firm brushing. Do not worry about catching any fleas yourself at this point, for any remaining will be dead. The process should be repeated two or three weeks later, though less thoroughness may be needed.

Kittens cannot be treated in this way, for the chemicals are too strong; also, the mother would lick the powder off and swallow it. Fleas on new kittens must be left for six or seven weeks, until the kittens are strong enough to stand the treatment, so isolate the cat family in one room with much powder on the floor. It is wise to take precautions by inspecting a pregnant cat for fleas two or three weeks before the kittens are due to be born.

Bedding The cat's bedding must be cleaned. All towels, cloths and newspaper must be removed and preferably destroyed, for the fleas breed, not on the cat, but in snug little dark and dusty corners. So put everything it uses in the house, such as a basket, out in the fresh air for a few hours if it cannot be washed or destroyed. Liberally sprinkle it with powder before putting new clean cloths or cushions inside. You may only need to do this once or twice in a normal cat's life, but examine its fur frequently. If you have more than one cat, or live in an area where your cat meets a lot of strays or dirty companions, it is possible for the whole house to be infested with fleas, so take action with your cat immediately you see any sign of them on him.

In the house If you are too late the fleas will lay eggs in any part of the house, under the carpets or anywhere that they

67

can remain undisturbed. Then they will come out and attack you. If you are unfortunate enough to suffer this, take thorough measures at once. Hang out every sheet and blanket from the beds; puff pest powder under every carpet and piece of lino in the house, under the stair carpet, in every corner, especially the dark and warm ones. Fleas rarely rise more than eight or ten inches from the ground, but you should puff the skirting boards, behind cupboards, inside low wardrobes. This must be done very thoroughly everywhere, using several packs of powder – one will treat an average-sized room. Leave the powder for a fortnight, then remove with a vacuum-cleaner. A slightly less intensive repeat performance after about six weeks will ensure that you are free of even the last trace of eggs.

Flea collars

There are flea collars on the market, for which the manufacturers make claims that I have never been able to prove. They maintain that a flea on a cat must move about the animal's body, especially to obtain moisture from the mouth and eyes. To do this they must pass the neck and thus cannot avoid touching a collar which is impregnated with a strong chemical which kills fleas but is harmless to cats.

The collar must be loose enough, however, for the cat to be able to free its head if it is caught in a bush or going through a small hole, so the collar may be lost after a few days. This seems an expensive way of keeping a cat free of fleas when a weekly brush-down, and an occasional slight dusting with powder, seems equally effective in normal conditions.

No other pests are common to cats. If you think your cat has a pest or other parasite you should consult a vet at once. One final word about fleas. It is comforting that they will not breed on your person or clothing. They breed and lay eggs outside the animal they live on and feed on, although they alight on people to feed on the blood through the skin. If you suspect fleas in the house, walk about with bare feet – they will jump on to your feet. You can easily catch them with a wet finger and thumb and drown them. They are not harmful if dealt with in this way.

Communicating and playing with your cat

Your voice The most important sound in your cat's life so far as you are concerned is your voice and the most important word for him *is* his own name. It is doubtful whether he knows that this is his name, though he may learn that one sound you make with your voice specially concerns him. So say it many times and in many ways. He will take notice of the tone of voice you use to say his name and will purr or cower, scoot, run to you or look enquiringly, according to your tone.

Do not worry too much about his understanding you. Just talk to him as often as possible and he will know that you are thinking about him; that will be enough for him. He will love it and grow closer to you as a result.

His voice You should listen to the many sounds your cat makes and try to understand their meaning. I have counted fifteen different sounds from one of my cats and each one meant something special. You may find that your cat has five or six distinct mews and miaows, a variety of squeaks and peeps which mean 'hello' or 'please' or 'PLEASE ! ! !', or 'let me i-i-i-i-n-n-n'.

He has growls for kittens, growls for humans, snarls for other cats, screeches for intruders and the noise he makes for his enemies cannot be spelled out at all. He has a number of different murmurs which might mean 'thank you for letting me in' or 'don't forget me and my dinner'. In fact, if you listen to *his* tone of voice you will discover many interpretations. One curious 'word' which seems common to cats is that little snicker or whimper which he makes with his trembling lower jaw when he sees a bird he cannot reach. I have heard dozens of cats make the same noise and it always meant 'bird'.

'Please let me in'

'Must I wait much longer?'

His expressions Your cat communicates as much with his face as with his voice, like you do. Watch him and see what he is trying to tell you with those subtle changes of expression. Notice how often he half closes his eyes to look up at you, flicks an ear, or lays it back; how he can open his eyes wide, sometimes enquiringly, sometimes apprehensively, sometimes in amazement.

His tail is interesting, for he expresses a lot with it. He will stick it straight up to tell you he is glad to see you, and swish it gently from side to side or flip a playful tail-tip when he is purring happily. Beware when he slashes it wildly about, for then he is telling you that unless you let him go immediately he will give you a taste of his claws. Kittens sometimes whizz their tails round and round like windmills when they are scared or over-excited.

Giving orders It is necessary to give orders to your cat that he will both understand and obey. To teach him these orders you must choose words which are short and clear and quite different from each other. Always use the same word for the same order and in the same circumstances. My present cat can understand OUT for 'go out of this room', DOWN for 'get down from the table or bed', NO (said most firmly if he considers disobeying) for 'don't do that', and that is his limit. He does not understand that SEPTI is his name (short for Septipuss) and comes for food, not when I call his name, but when he hears the clatter of his dishes or the fish pan.

Communication A good example of my cat's intelligent attempt to communicate, which has happened several times, is that, as soon as the fish pan boils on the cooker, if I am not in the room, Septi runs to me and mews loudly – even through a closed door.

Handling cats

Lifting a kitten You may have been told that the correct way to pick up a cat is by the scruff of its neck. This is wrong.

A kitten may be lifted in this way, for its weight is not too great. In fact, a mother cat carries her young so, although sometimes she will take the whole head of a

A brown Burmese being held safely and comfortably

kitten into her mouth to carry it. A full-grown cat is too heavy to be lifted like this.

Lifting a cat To lift a cat you should put one hand under the chest or front legs, and let it sit on the other hand. To carry a cat, or to hold it for some time, you should put your hands and arms in such a position that it can sit on one arm and put its front feet on the other; or so that it can lie on your arms with all four feet tucked underneath. The best way to make it stay in your arms is to ensure that it feels safe and comfortable there.

Do not hold it tightly for if it feels that it is trapped and being held prisoner, it will struggle to get free. Then you will feel its claws!

If you teach your cat to trust you and to feel safe in your hands, you will be able to walk around with him quite easily. Later, he may sit on your shoulder or even on the back of your neck. I have walked in the street many times with a cat on my shoulder, as traffic passed by, but she had learned to trust me, just as I had learned to trust her not to jump down at the wrong time.

Another cat frequently lay round my neck, with his paws down each side over my shoulders while I worked in the dark-room.

Holding by the neck However, there are some times when you might have to take a cat by the loose skin at the back of its neck: for instance, when a vet needs to inspect it or when you are going to do something to it which it will not like, such as rubbing pest powder into the fur or giving medicine. I believe that holding by the scruff of the neck is a mother's way of disciplining kittens, and also one cat's way of showing mastery over another cat, as when the male holds his female by the back of the neck.

So when you intend to discipline your kitten or young cat you may take him by this loose skin and hold it up. He will realise that he is helpless, and will feel cowed, knowing he is being dealt with sternly. His tail will curl up between his back legs and his face take on a sorrowful expression.

Occasionally, a kitten may be held by the scruff of its neck

When you are holding the cat for the vet, do so very firmly but not harshly. There is no need to be rough,

73

A mother cat carrying her kitten

or hurt him. Hold the loose skin with one hand and caress him with the other, while you talk to him. If it is necessary to pick up a cat with one hand only, place your open hand right under its chest and make sure you can lift it comfortably without clutching, so that it feels safe. Small hands may not be able to manage this.

Playing with your cat

A kitten starts to play at about the age of three weeks. From the first day he is merely experiencing a bewildering sequence of unknown events and sounds, until a few of them are repeated often enough to make the kitten realise that there is some sense in the pattern of the world around him. Confidence then begins to grow.

As he sees and feels the world of his own family and

Cats at play

bed and food, he finds some experiences more pleasurable than others. He begins to learn, to discover that he can move, that he can also make other things move. He begins to experiment. He extends a paw to investigate that object just in front of him, and finds that it is too far away to reach or nearer than he thought. He might find out that it is something soft or furry, or that it can move by itself, or that it bites or scratches. The kitten enjoys some of the things he does and tries to repeat them. He begins to play.

All play is a form of preparation for adult life. The kitten is first testing the world about him, then trying himself out. When, in his fourth or fifth week, he pushes his brother away and tries to sit on his sister, he is making his first moves in fun fighting that will very soon develop into that full-scale rough and tumble and, later still, into defensive scraps for food or mates or territory. He might start by tapping his mother's ear – the training that will fit him for encountering marauding dogs or rats or other animals.

He will run after a table-tennis-ball as part of his learning to hunt; he will climb trees or curtains as part of his learning to avoid an enemy. He will hide under the settee and whack your foot as you pass, just as his ancestors had to ambush their prey generations ago.

Playing with your kitten
When you play with your kitten, you should remember why he plays, and that he can only play in his own way; he cannot learn to play your way. He does not understand hide-and-seek as a game. He will play by hiding from you while you seek him but he will never seek you if you hide. If he cannot easily see, smell or hear you, he will give up and play with something else. If you chase him he will run away to hide but he will rarely chase you, for you are so much bigger than he is, too much like an overwhelming attacker. However, he will love to chase a ball of paper or a scrap of something pulled by a string. He will play with the string itself also, but must not be allowed to swallow it.

If you swing a piece of paper on a string very wildly, he will leap frantically from side to side, up and down, trying to catch his prey. He must succeed from time to time, or he will give up the game altogether, although I am sure he prefers the chase to the capture.

Two of his favourite playthings are your hand and his mother's tail. He will almost bite, not quite sinking in his teeth. He knows he could hurt, but will not do so deliberately and he will eventually learn to control his claws.

His mother will sit on a chair arm while her kittens fight and bite her tail as it dangles on the seat. She will gently wave it or flick it, as they jump and scramble about, loving this long, fluffy, soft, harmless plaything. It is a fascinating game to watch.

Toys A cotton-reel is another good toy and so is a small rag doll. Some firms produce special toys for cats and dogs with suitable meaty or fishy smells. These are either bags made from tough material with appropriate fillings which contain a substance with the required smell, or hard rubber-like toys which can be gnawed or thrown around, and have both smell and taste to interest the pet. They become very dirty but the best of them are washable. Loose bits should be removed so that they will not be swallowed. No toy should be small enough to go right into a cat's mouth, nor should it be breakable in such a way as to make swallow-sized pieces.

Playing with a young cat Many simple ways of playing with a young cat can be devised. Tear up a whole newspaper and spread the crumpled pieces on the floor. Bury the cat in them and he will rush in and out of the pile, popping up here and there. Or make a disordered heap of cardboard boxes and the cat will climb about happily, peeping out of each box in turn. Cats love a labyrinth.

If you allow it, your whole house will become your cat's playground; as he grows and learns his way round the rooms, he will chase his brothers at high speed, swishing round sharp corners, skidding on lino, braking on mats to stop on an exact spot or turning in the air as if blown back by a great gust of wind. During all this activity, he is preparing himself for that tiger-like life he would have led as a jungle creature, where he would have had to find his food, kill it, or defend himself, by sheer speed, stealth, strength and fitness.

He will keep up much of this play until he is a year or two old. For three or four years he will continue to play on his own occasionally, but unless you play with him sometimes he will give up altogether. At the age of about two, he will have learned that none of this play has taught him the skills he needs, for he is not a jungle creature. He will settle down to be a calmer, more sedate animal, not requiring speed and power.

Photographing cats

It is fun photographing cats. They are such excellent subjects and do so many lovely things that you can hardly fail to get something worth photographing. However, you rarely have much control over the picture itself; the model has a mind of his own and you have to take what is there – take it or leave it.

Equipment As you will not be buying equipment especially to take photographs of cats, you will use whatever you possess. An ordinary camera and lens will give many good pictures but they are likely to be rather small, for a cat is quite a small animal. If you have either a telephoto lens for photographing from a distance, or a close-up lens for getting close in to your subject, the work will be much easier. Indoors, flash equipment is almost essential, preferably electronic as the flash itself is much quicker than bulbs.

If you have a variable camera you should use the highest shutter speed possible for a moving cat, since movement, even so much as a thickness of a hair, can

make the picture blurred. At least 1/250th of a second is necessary. A running cat can reach up to 40 miles an hour in a sudden sprint.

On the other hand, to take a close-up of a resting cat you should use the smallest aperture possible to obtain adequate depth of field. Try f16 or f22. That means a slow shutter speed, of course.

The most important element in cat photography is patience. You can watch for a long time and no picture will materialise; put the camera down for a moment and the cat will leap into all sorts of fantastic gyrations and expressions. Keep trying. Do not expect a picture a minute – three or four an hour, perhaps. Sit with your eye to the focussing view-finder, trained on the cat or its family, then wait. There is no picture at all, then suddenly, there is – SNAP.

You can take some steps to guide the activities of the cat and create certain pictures almost at will, if you think them out in advance and enlist the help of a friend.

Set the camera on a table or tripod, focussed on a spot on the floor. Hold it very still.

Let the cat see a tiny piece of rag on the end of a length of cotton. Tease the cat a little with it, until he wants to chase it, then trail the rag across the spot you have focussed on, and SNAP. The cat will pass the spot in an interesting position. Or swing the rag in the air at a distance exactly measured from the camera and the cat will jump and leap after it. As it leaps – SNAP. Electronic flash will stop the cat's movement in mid-flight.

A good device is to put something strange on the floor at the point you have focussed on. As the cat stealthily sneaks up to sniff it, you will have a good picture already, if you want it. If you wait, just as it puts its nose to the object, ask a friend to clap his hands loudly – and SNAP, you will have a picture of a cat leaping backwards in the air.

Photographing kittens Leave the kittens without milk for a short while, then put a bowl of milk on a low table (I prefer a bed for height) with just one kitten. The others will hear it

lapping and come for their share. The resulting scrum makes a good picture.

If you want fighting pictures you will need the help of two friends. Drape a white sheet over a settee and throw a couple of kittens on top of each other in the middle of it. Focus on that point and every time they run away, your friends should put them back on the settee. You will find them scrapping time and again and you will get a lovely set of pictures.

'Arty' pictures   You must plan these beforehand. Look for silhouettes, back-lighting or interesting settings. For this type of picture indoors, use a small room and use 'bounce' flash;

that is, turn your flash to the ceiling or opposite wall. It is necessary to open the aperture two stops. This kind of lighting is more natural.

Mother and kittens
To take a picture of a cat carrying its kittens, you must do so when the kittens are over two weeks old, not before, or you may distress both kitten and mother. Make preparations carefully. Choose a good place for the picture and focus on that spot, leaving your camera ready on a tripod, a box or a chair. Carry one kitten from the basket to a place at the opposite side of the chosen spot. Soon the mother will hear her kitten calling and will go for it, pick it up and carry it straight back to the basket.

If you have chosen the place well, she will pass straight in front of your camera and – SNAP. A good location is the top of the stairs; another is an open doorway, or near the basket itself. In fact, you could put two kittens there and, as the first kitten is carried back, you will realise where you should choose to take the picture of the second kitten being carried.

Do not do this more than twice or the mother will be upset and puzzled.

Yawning cats If you want to photograph yawning cats, try this method. Sit in a warm room with your cat, stroking and caressing it until it settles on a chair or a suitable

place. Soon it will doze. Focus on it, then make a tiny clicking or squeaking noise. The cat will lift its head, see that nothing is happening, yawn and doze again.

Taking portraits Try going behind the cat and calling to it. As it turns its head, SNAP. On the other hand, you may want to take it 'straight' but not asleep. To make it 'sit' for you, ask a friend to help.

The friend should hold the cat on a stool gently but firmly, talking to it, reassuring it, *asking* it to be obliging, stroking it slowly. He should slowly withdraw his hands and the cat will almost certainly sit still for quite a long time waiting to see what is going to happen. You will have plenty of time to take the portrait.

Kittens Cover the open top of a shallow box with a large sheet of white paper, in the middle of which is a hole about four inches across. Put two or three kittens inside the box, focus on the hole and wait. In time a head is sure to pop up. You can take a series of pictures as all the kittens try to clamber out.

Put a kitten in an unusual place and watch its re-
actions – on a step-ladder, amongst flowers, in tall grass,
near to a goldfish bowl (the fish will be quite safe), or
into a paper bag. Snap his expression when he first
touches water.

I hope you will never dress up a cat, or tie ribbons
on him. His natural appearance is better. A cat is too
dignified an animal to be made ridiculous and quite
beautiful enough without decorations. Only lack of
appreciation makes a photographer use gimmicks.

Welfare organisations

There are many organisations with charitable foundations and aims which can help you with your cat.

If you would like the companionship of other people who are interested in cats generally, or in one particular breed, you will find details of Cat Clubs later in this chapter. Welfare organisations deal with all aspects of the health and happiness of cats and other animals and help to prevent distress and cruelty.

R.S.P.C.A. *The Royal Society for the Prevention of Cruelty to Animals*, The Manor House, Horsham, Sussex, will deal with any complaints about cruelty or neglect. The Society issues booklets on the care of cats, a newspaper called *RSPCA Today*, and a magazine, *Animal Ways*, for young people. There are fully trained inspectors in most towns, whose addresses can be found in the telephone directory or obtained from the police. These inspectors will investigate any cases of cruelty or neglect, give help in accidents or rescue cats from anywhere they may be trapped. They will try to help in finding homes for strays or unwanted kittens but, if they cannot do so, they will arrange for the animals to be put down. Thousands of kittens are destroyed every year. The Society also operates treatment clinics – for a donation.

The Animal Welfare Trust   *The Animal Welfare Trust* is an offshoot of the *British Union for Abolition of Vivisection*, B.U.A.V. The address is 47 Whitehall, London SW1. This organisation, too, will investigate cases of distress reported to it and will help to find homes. In addition, they catch stray cats and, after sterilising them, return them to their natural habitat. This helps to reduce their number.

P.D.S.A.   *The People's Dispensary for Sick Animals*, South Street, Dorking, Surrey, is also a national organisation. This body specialises in providing medical care for sick animals of all kinds but it is intended only for people who cannot afford a vet's fee for their pet. The clinics in various parts of Britain treat about a million cases a year and rely entirely on voluntary donations. The P.D.S.A. publishes a magazine for children called *Animals' Magazine*.

N.C.D.L.   *The National Canine Defence League* caters primarily for dogs at their various centres though, of course, they deal with other animals. The address is 10 Seymour Street, Portman Square, London W1. The work with cats is mainly at their clinics, where vets treat the pets of people who genuinely cannot afford professional fees. The clinics are at Lillie Road, Fulham; Cherry Orchard Road, Croydon; Preston Park, Brighton; also, a mobile clinic which visits Camberwell and Hackney in London. All the clinics are well-established and have provided treatment for a vast number of animals.

(A vet from the N.C.D.L. assisted the author with the section on Common Ailments in chapter 7.)

C.P.L. *The Cats' Protection League and Tailwavers* is the only national organisation which undertakes the specific job of looking after the interests of cats. The address is 29 Church Street, Slough, Bucks. The League investigates reports of experiments in animal laboratories, sponsors twenty-four centres, some of which run clinics, and seeks out colonies of cats that are stray or needing rescue or other attention. Cats are often nursed back to health, sent to good homes, or neutered and returned to their chosen homes. This League was founded over forty years ago and depends, as most others do, on voluntary donations and legacies.

The Blue Cross The name of the organisation shows that it is an animal society similar to the Red Cross which helps people. It was started over eighty years ago and incorporates Our Dumb Friends' League. Its half-yearly publication, *Blue Cross Illustrated*, is one of the most attractive available and has many colour pictures. There is a smaller publication for young people.

The Blue Cross is concerned with all birds and animals, including cats. In Hugh Street, Victoria, London SW1, there is a very modern Animals' Hospital, with a vet on call day and night as well as night staff. A good Home of Rest for cats is situated in Northiam, Sussex, centred round an old oast-house. There are Blue Cross Hospitals in Hammersmith, London, and Grimsby, Lincolnshire, and the Cats' Home just outside Cambridge is said to be one of the most modern anywhere. There are clinics and centres in various other places; one at Willesden, London deals with welfare boarding for the pets of old folk who are going on holiday or into hospital. There is an Animals' Home in Chalfont St Peter, Buckinghamshire, with a large cattery, and another in Felixstowe. Visitors are welcome at all these places – but they prefer to know in advance.

Other Organisations Many smaller organisations exist all over the country to deal with strays, to find homes, to offer medical help and generally to make sure no one feels unable to cope with a pet problem. Two good examples are:

The Margaret Green Foundation Trust and the *Cats Any Time Service*.

The Margaret Green Foundation Trust

The Margaret Green Foundation Trust (no relation to the author) has a sanctuary at Church Knowle, Wareham, Dorset. It looks after many kinds of animals either until natural death comes or a willing owner is found. Before they pass animals to a new home, the Welfare Officer of the Trust pays a visit to the home first to see that all will be well and keeps in touch after the transfer. No animal is put to sleep unless it is incurably ill. Cats have complete freedom in the sanctuary grounds and there are always many around. People here are very keen that cats should be neutered to prevent haphazard breeding. This is a registered charity and relies largely on donations.

Cats Any Time Service

Cats Any Time Service in Orpington, Kent, is run by a group of people who decided to deal with cat welfare in the area. They specialise in seeking out the cats that have settled in colonies of strays, collecting the kittens before they begin to breed, neutering them and returning them to the colony, thus reducing the number of strays. A local hospital was faced with such a problem and this service dealt with two hundred kittens in a year. Funds are raised by coffee mornings and jumble sales. One organiser is Mrs M. Howe, 66 Lynwood Grove, Orpington, Kent.

Cat Clubs

There are three kinds of cat club : pet clubs, National Cat Club and breed clubs.

Pet Clubs

These are usually small and local, consisting of a group of people who love cats, and enjoy sharing the pleasure they derive from their pets. Clubs of this kind may be centred round a school or a church, or even a couple of streets. All members are usually amateurs and pedigree cat owners do not often join them.

If there are sufficient members, they can buy food in bulk and more cheaply, invite vets and other experts to give talks at meetings or arrange their own small local shows, with outside judges. These clubs can be good places for children to learn to treat their pets seriously and sensibly. Neighbouring cat owners should be able to tell you where to find such a club or you could form one yourself, among your friends.

Area and County Pet Clubs These are much larger versions of the local pet clubs and more ambitiously organised. Some may have paid officials to run them. They have good standing among pedigree cat owners and establish their reputations by holding shows of their own. Some of these are championship shows which earn for prizewinners the right to enter top-class shows. They usually have pet classes in their shows. Sometimes they sponsor prizes and classes in shows other than their own, especially in the National Cat Club Show.

The areas specified in these clubs' titles are not always rigidly adhered to, for members are accepted from a much wider area than the name indicates. Membership can cost as little as 25p a year, after an initial enrolment fee, or up to £1 or more. On entering a show an owner has to pay a fee for each class.

Some clubs issue magazines, mostly duplicated Newsletters.

It would be difficult to give a complete list of all of these clubs, but below is a selection of clubs for different parts of the country.

National Cat Club This is the major organisation for all pedigree cat and pet owners in Britain. It has a number of committees for various purposes and its focal point is the annual show at Olympia in December. It is the Cat Fancy's equivalent to Crufts of the dog world. Thousands of cats take part.

No Best in Show is named but Best in Breed is chosen for each breed. The Honorary Secretary is Mrs Gowdy, Summers Lodge, Summerleys Road, Princes Risborough, Bucks. The Honorary Secretary of The Pet Cat Section is Mrs E. Nash, Catwyck Motel, Ashton, Nr. Helston, Cornwall.

At least one visit to the National Show is a great experience for cat owners, whether pedigree or pet owner.

Other Clubs   *Southern Counties Cat Club*
North East Scotland Cat Club
Kentish Cat Club
Kensington Kitten and Neuter Cat Club
Three Counties Cat Society (Dorset, etc.)
Yorkshire County Cat Club
Northern Counties Cat Club
Notts and Derbyshire Cat Club
Croydon Cat Club
Bedford and District Cat Club
Lancashire & North West Counties Cat Club
Suffolk and Norfolk Cat Club
Coventry and Leicester Cat Club
Midland Counties Cat Club
Hertfordshire and Middlesex Cat Club
Cheshire Area Cat Club
Edinburgh and East of Scotland Cat Club
Kentish Cat Society
Scottish Cat Club
Wessex Cat Club

Breed Clubs   By far the most important clubs in the country for owners of pedigree cats are those catering specifically for the various breeds. They help to set standards and to foster the welfare of the breed so that bad points are not propagated indiscriminately. They spread information about disease likely to affect the breed and do all they can to improve the breed.

They also publish literature on these subjects for the benefit of members and issue periodical bulletins with news of shows, winners, cats at stud, and illustrations of quality cats. They sponsor their own shows, usually open to non-members with cats of that breed, and the best of these clubs are qualified to hold Championship Shows which give status to the winners. They also sponsor classes at other championship shows, giving prizes, rosettes and winners' cards.

One or two breed clubs participate in International Cat Fancy activities.

These clubs will accept novices and advise about

breeding and stud cats; they understand that everyone starts as a novice, so are ready to help in many ways. They advise about forthcoming litters and where a kitten of this breed can be purchased. Here is a list of the most important of them:

Abyssinian C.C. Mrs S. Bullock, Seal Point, Old Acre Lane, BRACTON, Stafford

Black & White C.C. Mrs J. Crockart, 152 Bramhall Lane, Davenport, STOCKPORT, Cheshire

Birman Cat Club Miss R. E. Brown, The Annexe, Castle Lea, Crete Road West, FOLKESTONE, Kent

Blue Persian C.S. R. A. Cordell, 69 The Meadows, Ingrave, BRENTWOOD, Essex

Blue-Pointed Siamese C.C. Mrs G. Lait, 25 The Parade, DUDLEY, Worcs.

Burmese C.C. Miss M. R. Silverman, Flat 6, 25 Shepherds Hill, LONDON N.6

Capital Long-Hair C. Association Mrs V. Croysdill, Cheese House, Britford, SALISBURY, Wilts.

Chinchilla, Silver Tabby, and Smoke Cat Society Mrs M. Greenwood, 73 Bassingham Road, EARLESFIELD, London SW18

Chocolate-Pointed Siamese C.C. Mrs A. Weldin, Netherwoods, Middleton Road, CAMBERLEY, Surrey

Colourpoint, Rex-coated and Any Other Variety C.C. Mrs A. Mackenzie, Ludgrove Hall, Games Road, COCKFOSTERS, Herts.

Foreign Short-Hair C.C. Miss M. May, 265 Green Lanes, LONDON N13

Foreign White Cat Fanciers' Assn. Mr J. Mais, Chaisley, South Cliff, EASTBOURNE, Sussex

Foreign White Cat Society Mrs H. Phillips, 4 Green Bank, Woodside Avenue, LONDON N12

North of Britain Long-Hair Cat Club Mrs E. Tillotson, 32 Bradley Road, Silsden, KEIGHLEY, Yorks.

Red Point and Tortie Point Siamese C.C. Miss J. May, 265 Green Lanes, LONDON N.13

Rex C.C. Mrs B. Lyon, 8 Godwin Close, Grovehurst, SITTINGBOURNE, Kent

Siamese Cat Club (this is the largest breed club in Europe) Mrs M. Dunhill, The Garth, High Lane, HASLEMERE, Surrey

Short-Haired C.S. of Great Britain and Manx Club Inc. Mrs S. Beever, Poplars House Farm, Fenwick, ASKERN, Nr. Doncaster, Yorks.

Tabby C.C. Ralph Chapman, Karnak, Mannington, WIMBORNE, Dorset

White Persian C.C. Mrs I. O'Donnell, Atlanta House, Hockering, DEREHAM, Norfolk

These clubs should cover every breed you are likely to want for a pet. Some special breeds of cats are very expensive to buy and they are expensive to breed because the stud cats are few and, therefore, more in demand. Inevitably, they attract higher fees. Clubs for these cats have not been included in the list.

The best source of information about other clubs is the Secretary of the National Cat Club.

Index